Dixit Poems

Laura Brown

BookLeaf
Publishing

India | USA | UK

Presentation by *BookLeaf Publishing*

Web: www.bookleafpub.com

E-mail: info@bookleafpub.com

ISBN: 9789357449175

First edition 2022

DEDICATION

For my Sam.

Autumn winds

The old man walked through the wilds, leaning on his stick as he went. The wind blew between the furrowed hills around him, swirling and catching at his leaves until slowly, one by one, they rushed off into it's dancing, playful eddies, leaving him behind. The stick he leant on was sturdy and knobbed, as old as he was himself and he trusted it with his weight each time his weary steps plodded onwards. The wind grew around him and his leaves began to fall faster, catching and tugging at his limbs and his face. He lifted an arm to shield his eyes from the glow of the dying light ahead.

Although he was weary, the old man knew that he could not stop, his journey was to go on farther still. His task to walk around the world, bringing blazing orange in his wake. He trudged up the rounded hills and stopped, there to catch his breath for a second. As he stood, silhouetted against the fiery sky, he turned his head one last time to look down into the valley.

Ah yes, he thought, Autumn has come at last.

Ballet shoes

The shoes danced on. After the clamour of the audience had gone home with their coats and bags, their applause and exclamations. The shoes danced on in an empty theatre. After the lights were dimmed and the engineers long in their beds. The shoes danced on in a darkened corner. After the musicians ceased to play and the instruments lay dormant in their crushed velvet casings. The shoes danced on to a silent stage. After the tired ankles and bruised toes had moved out into the city streets. The shoes danced on.

Theirs was a brief existence, akin to a mayfly. For what were they really but a tool for the dancer, an appendage to the music? They danced on while they could, and when the music was gone from them, the life faded, their brief work done. The shoes, at last, were still.

The stone king

The stone king stood on his plinth and watched the world from on high where he had stood for years gone by and would stand for years to come. When he was first carved from the huge slab of stone, he had been hopeful and naïve, thinking that this was a good world and he had been put there in the town square to reflect that goodness, to remember the knights and kings of long ago. He later thought that he might inspire the people of the town to become better, he stood straight and tireless, hoping that his noble image might recall to their minds some of the honour of long ago. Those thoughts had now passed. The stone king had come to realise over the years that there would always be pain and suffering. He saw the hungry children searching for fallen crumbs underneath the market stalls each week, he heard the birds chattering about the seamstresses and washerwomen who worked so hard their fingers would bleed at the slightest touch and still they could not rest for there was always more work to be done. He knew now that he could not help these people, the best he could do was offer some small shelter from the wind to those who huddled round his feet during

the cold winter months. He had grown used to
the cries of the cold and the shivers of the
hungry in his years standing in the square but his
heart had not grown hard, though the rest of him
was cold and firm, still his heart beat warm
within him. His was a gentle heart and it bled
with each and every tear his people shed. Until
the little boy with the icy cold fingers sat on his
feet and looked up at the stone king with such
hope in his eyes. The stone king wished more
that anything that he could help him. The little
boy fell asleep still perched on the cold stone
and the stone king, frustrated that he was unable
even to warm this small child, began to cry. As
the tears fell down his cheeks he felt warmth and
life inside him. He reached out and cradled the
boy to his chest. At last, thought the king, here
is love.

Footprints

He followed the footprints back through his front garden to see where they had come from. But they didn't stop there. He followed them down his street and around the corner. He followed them back through the park past the empty swings but still they didn't stop there. He followed the footprints down the path to the hills, over bumps and ruts in the road, down to the beach they went. But they didn't stop there. He followed the footprints back across the sand to see where they had come from. He followed them until they disappeared into the ocean itself, imprints upon the sea floor. But they didn't stop there.

A new perspective

The little doll looked carefully around. Left, right, she was alone at last. She tiptoed to the edge of her bedroom where the floor stopped and the big space began, listening carefully all the while. Still there was no one. She did not remember how long she had lived in her little house. All she knew was that she had woken up this morning and seen for the first time the vast empty space before her, she could no longer see the fourth wall of her bedroom. To begin with she had wandered from room to room aghast at the missing walls and the newfound space. She had cowered behind the kitchen table for a short while before curiosity had overtaken her. She had never thought of a life outside her little house, never in her mind conceived that there might be a space so large. But here it was. And it was with excitement that the little doll sat on the edge of her bedroom floor and slipped off into the unknown.

The cellist

She played her strings boldly, the music flowing from deep within her soul. It poured out from her very being and saturated the world around her. Every feeling, every thought, all was possessed by the music, widening, stretching out as it reached for those around her. As they listened, they began to recognise in the music words and sentiments they themselves held dear. It swirled around them and teased of a higher way. A way hitherto unknown. They let the music lift them gently and encourage them on as they climbed to her heights. Onward and ever upward they flew, finding meaning and solace in those beautiful notes until they and she were one with the sound, and all was bliss.

Standing in a sea of sunflowers

Standing in a sea of sunflowers
Here I stand
Here I stand
All day I stand in the sunflowers
All day I stand
All day I stand
In the dark I am protection
I am their guard
I am their guard
I point the way to heaven
I am their guide
I am their guide
The birds come wheeling round
Cawing loud
Cawing loud
I stand here proud and tall
Above them all
Above them all
A smile is fixed upon my face
I fix a smile
I fix a smile
Although it covers my disgrace

All covered up
All covered up
From day to year to month I'll stand
Here I stand
Here I stand
Forever in my field of sunflowers
Forevermore
Forevermore

The dreamer

The dreamer chipped away at the clouds in the sky. He worked with hammer and chisel, for clouds were not, as most people believed, fluffy creations of mist and snow. Rather they were the barrier between the earth and the sky, the only decoration of the blue expanse above. And as the only ornament, they could not be simply blown into place, each and every one was carefully planned and chipped into the elegant and everchanging shapes that those below would seldom look up to or notice. The dreamer sighed, his was a lonely job he thought as he leant back to survey his work. For the clouds would change again in a moment, there would be no rest for him as he chased these white pilgrims across the sky and formed them into the shapes of his dreams.

The hourglass

I thought back on my life, the good and the bad and wondered about the young girl I could still see, still feel. Was it she who shaped me or I who formed her? It was impossible to tell. So many moments had passed between the two of us, I only knew that we were bound together, trapped in the never ending hourglass. Beginning and end were lost on me. I could see the girl, elegant and carefree, dancing as she became, with each passing tick of the clock, more like me. At least in body. In mind, I seemed to become more like her, the cares of the years worn away until I could dance with her grace again. At least in mind.

The daisy

The daisy had grown up through a tiny gap in the cracked city pavement. She huddled in a corner as the hurried feet passed her by in their thousands, sometimes she thought she could feel the very ground shaking as they rushed onward trampling everything in their path. She reached up and felt her slim white petals fading with the day. She thought of gardens fragrant and magnificent, she imagined cliffs by the sea and all the honeyed mass of golden gorse in bloom, for these things she had never seen and never would. Despite her solitude she stood tall, her task was to bring beauty where she could and she would certainly do her best to bring her small beauty to the little crack in the bustling city street she called home.

Sunshine

The sun peeked out her head, eager to shine on the good and the bad alike. But when she opened her eyes and looked down onto the people they hurried to and fro, not bothering to look up. Not one of them stopped to enjoy the warm morning glow. The sun frowned and started her climb into the sky. Maybe the next town would be pleased to see her. However the next town was even worse, the people hurried from one doorstep to the next, ducking into shadows, not wanting to linger in the sun's yellow light.

It was the same in each new town that she shone upon and the sun was dismayed. It hadn't always been like this, the people used to be glad to see her, they would lift up their eyes to wave their hands and smile at her. When did everything change?

She continued on her journey across the sky, no longer bothering to look down at the people.

She would come back tomorrow and shine as bright as she could and maybe then, the people would love her again.

The sun carried on through the sky, not looking down until something caught her eye. There were bright colours down below and the patches of colour were moving, weaving into and around one another. She had never seen anything like it. It even looked like these colours had legs and were scurrying around the cars and buildings down below. As she leaned in for a closer look, one of the pockets of colour moved aside and there, smiling up at her, was a face. The sun couldn't understand it, were these some new creatures that she hadn't seen before? Again she leaned down and this time, more faces came out of the colour to look up at her. The people (for they were indeed people) were closing up their little patches of colour and smiling at the clear blue sky. 'How nice to see the sun' they exclaimed to one another and took down their umbrellas. They turned their faces to the sky and the sun shone brighter than ever. In her mind, all was right with the world once again.

Choices

The caterpillar set out on his journey, not knowing what lay ahead. He did not know what choices he would make or what possibilities might spring from those decisions. He did not know if there would be danger or sorrow, laughter or delight. But still he went on, as bold as he could muster. For surely starting the journey was better than standing still.

Peace at last

Fear held court over the prison, rage his constant
friend and advisor. Sorrow dwelt in the corners
of the yard and hopelessness crouched in dark
hallways. Anguish was all too present and
torment permeated the very air of the cells.
Until the innocent man came.
He said no to fear, bid farewell to sadness and
anger, ignored denial and disbelief, shock was
pushed aside, grief abandoned.
In his solitary cell at the end of the corridor he
stayed. 'Here' said peace 'is my domain'.

The toyshop window

The toys gathered in the window, looking out onto the hustle and bustle of the busy city street that swept past their front door and on into the unknown. They oohed and aahed at the sights and sounds of the people going past. The business men in their suits and hats, the old ladies gossiping on the corner and the children, especially the children. They skipped past the window wearing all the colours of the rainbow, whether it was rain or shine and peered in at the dolls and planes and cars and stuffed animals. There was a great kerfuffle whenever a child pulled their parents by the hand into the toyshop and the toys would gather round the front of the window display elbowing one another to get the best view. And all the while one thought echoed around their heads 'will they choose me this time, have they come for me?'

The first map

Back when trees could walk and stones could talk. The voyager ship traversed the seas, charting the world where none had gone before. Each new country was an opportunity, each new ocean an adventure. As the ship passed by it left behind it a golden line as of a thread charting where it had travelled. These lines began to knit themselves together with the colours and textures of each new landmass reflected in the rich tapestry. The ship sailed on chasing new horizons and the map was knitted in its wake.

An arch of sky

The builders cheered as the first spot of sky showed through the hole in the brickwork. That small unwavering patch of blue seemed to spur them on and they worked feverishly all that day and into the next, eager to uncover some more of the tantalising expanse.

Slowly the gap widened and the bricks were pushed aside to unveil a swathe of blue with two perfectly formed fluffy white clouds (which everybody agreed was the just the right number). The edges of the brickwork were neatened up into a pleasing arch shape and the builders and their families all gathered round to celebrate the stretch of sky that they had uncovered.

Nobody thought to question whether the sky was real. After all, who can argue with a person who thinks they are free?

A field of poppies

There was a rustling in the grass. The poppies were awakening for the day, stretching their stalks, opening their leaves to the warm summer sun. The wind whistled playfully between their stems, causing them to sway and dance in the breeze. As they awoke, the poppies gradually became aware of something else, a new flower in their field. The knowledge rippled out from the centre and distilled itself among the flowers. They whispered and hustled to each other. Who was this newcomer? What could it possibly be doing in their field? All day they whispered and wondered to themselves about this new flower. Finally, as night fell and the poppies dropped off to sleep one by one, closing their crimson petals and bowing their heads, the new flower, draped in silver under the moonlight, lifted her head and opened herself to the stars. She did this but once in a hundred years. For she was older by far than the poppies and the grass of the field which is here today and gone tomorrow. She seldom noticed what surrounded her in her field, it was ever changing, she was still. She looked up to the moon and found her one true friend. The only thing in this world as unchanging as she.

The knight's tale

The knight galloped through the storybook on his faithful steed, defeating foes on the battlefield page after page, riding by obstacles large and small and beating aside his enemies with a mere bat of his sword. After all, he was the hero and so he sped on through the chapters, sentence after glorious sentence until all of a sudden he stopped. What was this? A new opponent creeping through the pages, reaching out for him with long green tentacles. He stopped in horror as his horse reared at this new threat. Perhaps this was not his story after all.